I want this book to put a smile on
your face. I want it to remind you that
you have been on my mind. And I want
it to help you remember — every time
you see it in the days yet to be —
that this book was given to you just
because... you're very special to me.

Blue Mountain Arts®

Best-Selling Titles

Been There, Done That, Doing It Better!
By Natasha Josefowitz

A Daughter Is Life's Greatest Gift

For My Wonderful Mother

For You, My Soul Mate
By Douglas Pagels

*Keep Believing in Yourself
and Your Dreams*

The Path to Success Is Paved with Positive Thinking
By Wally Amos with Stu Glauberman

The Promises of Marriage

A Son Is Life's Greatest Gift

The Strength of Women

Take Time for You
By M. Butler and D. Mastromarino

Today, I Will...
By James Downton, Jr.

*A True Friend
...Is Someone Just like You*
By BJ Gallagher

To Someone
Who Is
Very Special
to Me

Douglas Pagels

Blue Mountain Press™
Boulder, Colorado

Library of Congress Control Number: 2009905926
ISBN: 978-1-59842-444-7

Certain trademarks are used under license.
Blue Mountain Press is registered in U.S. Patent and Trademark Office.

Printed in China.
First Printing: 2009

Blue Mountain Arts, Inc.
P.O. Box 4549, Boulder, Colorado 80306

Contents

Has Anyone Ever Told You This?

Has anyone ever told you what a
wonderful person you are?

I hope so! I hope you've been
    told dozens of times...
        because you are just amazing.

And just in case you haven't heard
those words in a while,
I want you to hear them now.

You deserve to know that...

It takes someone special to do what you do. It takes someone rare and remarkable to make the lives of everyone around them nicer, brighter, and more beautiful. It takes someone who has a big heart and a caring soul. It takes someone who's living proof of how precious a person can be.

It takes someone... just like you.

A Little Story About "You and Me"

Me: So lucky to have this special connection!
You: The wonderful person I'm so thankful for.

Me: Someone who means well, but doesn't
always get it right.
You: Someone who gives my life so many
smiles and so much encouragement.

Me: A little insecure, a little uncertain, a little
crazy sometimes.
You: A huge help and a calming influence... all
the time.

You: Know what's going on inside me better
     than anyone.
Me: There isn't anybody else I can trust like this
    and no one I feel so comfortable turning to.

You: On a scale of 1 to 10, with 10 being the
    best, at least a 20.
Me: Counting my blessings and hearing your
    name come up so many times.

You: A joy to be with, to think of, and just to
    talk to.
Me: So incredibly glad... there's you.

20 Beautiful Things That Are True About You

You are something — and someone — very special. You really are. No one else in this entire world is exactly like you. You're a one-of-a-kind treasure, uniquely here in this space and time.

You are here to shine in your own wonderful way, sharing your smile in the best way you can and remembering all the while that a little light somewhere makes a brighter light everywhere. You can — and you do — make a wonderful contribution to this world, and there are so many beautiful things about you.

You have qualities within you that many people would love to have, and those who really and truly know you are so glad that they do...

You have a big heart and a good and sensitive soul. You are gifted with thoughts and ways of seeing things that only special people know. You know that life doesn't always play by the rules but that, in the long run, everything will work out. You understand that you and your actions are capable of turning anything around — and that joys once lost can always be found.

There is a resolve and an inner reserve of strength in you that few ever get to see. You have so many treasures within — those you're only beginning to discover... and all the ones you're already aware of.

Never forget what a treasure you are. That special person in the mirror may not always get to hear all the compliments you so sweetly deserve, but
you are so worthy of
such an abundance
...of friendship, joy, and love.

This Is Your Reminder

Every time you glance at this book, whether the day has been pleasant and easy or difficult and demanding, I want this to be your reminder that your presence in the world is always a wonderful thing. You are so deserving of every happiness I can possibly wish, and I constantly find myself thinking of you and wishing you knew about the smiles you inspire.

I want you to come home to these words in all the seasons ahead. And I want you to feel a glow in your heart just from knowing that you never, ever have to wonder if you're in someone's thoughts or if there's anybody out there who truly and lovingly appreciates you, because...

This book is always going to be here to tell you how much... I do.

Do You Know How Important You Are to Me?

I know you probably wonder
from time to time
what you mean to me.
So I'd like to share this thought
with you, to tell you that
you mean the world to me.

Think of something you couldn't live without
    ...and multiply it by a hundred.
Think of what happiness means to you
    ...and add it to the feeling you get
    on the best days you've ever had.

Add up all your best feelings
    and take away all the rest
    ...and what you're left with is
    exactly how I feel about you.

You matter more to me than you can
    imagine and much more than I'll ever
    be able to explain.

24 Things to Always Remember... and One Thing to Never Forget

Your presence is a present to the world.
You're unique and one of a kind.
Your life can be what you want it to be.
Take the days just one at a time.

Count your blessings, not your troubles.
You'll make it through whatever comes along.
Within you are so many answers.
Understand, have courage, be strong.

Don't put limits on yourself.
So many dreams are waiting to be realized.
Decisions are too important to leave to chance.
Reach for your peak, your goal, your prize...

Nothing wastes more energy than worrying.
The longer one carries a problem,
   the heavier it gets.
Don't take things too seriously.
Live a life of serenity, not a life of regrets.

Remember that a little love goes a long way.
Remember that a lot... goes forever.
Remember that friendship is a wise investment.
Life's treasures are people... together.

Realize that it's never too late.
Do ordinary things in an extraordinary way.
Have health and hope and happiness.
Take the time to wish upon a star.

And don't ever forget...
for even a day...
how very special you are.

Thoughts I'd Love to Share with You

You are so important to my days —
and so essential to the smile
    within me.
That certain space where our lives
overlap is the place that brings me
the most understanding,
    the most peace,
the nicest memories, and a joy that
    comes to my heart so constantly.

Because you're so important to me,
I want your life to be such a wonderful one.
I wish you peace, deep within your soul;
joyfulness in the promise of each new day;
stars to reach for, dreams to come true,
and memories more beautiful
     than words can say...

I wish you friends close at heart,
    even over the miles,
and loved ones — the best treasures
    we're blessed with.

I wish you present moments to live in,
    one day at a time;
serenity, with its wisdom;
    courage, with its strength;
and new beginnings, to give life a
    chance to really shine.

I wish you understanding
    of how special you really are
and a journey, safe from the storms and
    warmed by the sun.

I wish you a path to wonderful things;
an invitation to the abundance
    life brings;
and an angel watching over,
    for all the days to come.

For You

I don't know exactly what it is... but there is something very special about you.

It might be all the things I see on the surface: Things that everyone notices and admires about you. Qualities and capabilities. Your wonderful smile, obviously connected to a warm and loving heart. It might be all the things that set you apart from everyone else.

Maybe it's the big things: The way you never hesitate to go a million miles out of your way to do what's right. The way your todays help set the stage for so many beautiful tomorrows. Or maybe it's the little things: Words shared heart to heart. An unspoken understanding. Sharing seasons. Making some very wonderful memories. The joys of two people just being on the same page in each other's history...

If I could ever figure out all the magic that makes you so special, I'd probably find out that it's a combination of all these things — blended together with the best this world has to offer...

Friendship and love. Dreams come true. Strong feelings. Gentle talks. Listening...

...laughing and simply knowing someone whose light shines brighter than any star.

You really are amazing.

And I feel very lucky to have been given the gift of knowing how special you are.

You Are So Deserving

You are so deserving of every good
thing and every brighter day that
could ever be wished.

I hope all the things you long for will
find their way into your life.

May the days be good to you:
comforting more often than crazy
and giving more often than taking.

May the passing seasons make sure that any
    heartaches are replaced with a million smiles
    and that any hard journeys eventually
    turn into nice, easy miles that take you
    everywhere you want to go.

May your dreams do their absolute
    best to come true...

May your heart be filled with the kindness of friends, the caring of everyone you love, and the richness of memories you wouldn't trade for anything.

May life's little worries always stay small.

May you get a little closer every day to any goals you want to achieve.

May any changes be good ones and any
   challenges turn out to be for the better.

May you find time to do the things
   you've always wanted to do!

And may you be happy...
   forever.

Someone Will Always Be Thankful for You

Someone will always be thankful for you.

Someone will always cherish
the warmth of your smile and
the happiness in your heart.

Someone wants to always be close enough
to care in every way and to treasure
each and every day spent together.

Someone will always keep you lovingly in mind and will welcome every opportunity to find you in happy thoughts.

Someone will always know that life is good because of you and that tomorrow has a bright and shining hope that wouldn't be there if you weren't here today...

Someone will always try to find the words
to thank you for filling life with dreams
come true and beautiful memories.

Someone will always be thankful for you.

...And that someone
will always be me.

In Every Way

In big ways, in small ways,
in every single way...
the people who take the time
to go out of their way
to brighten the lives of others
are the ones who deserve
the sweetest thanks of all.

Priceless Moments

I wouldn't trade the days
    I've spent with you for anything.

Well... maybe just one thing.

A million more just like them.

If I Could

If I could have a wish come true, I'd wish
for every day of your life to be blessed with
some special gift that warms your heart,
some wonderful smile that
    touches your soul,
        and so many things that simply
            take your breath away.

I Care So Much About You

I care about you
  more than I can say.
And that caring and that feeling
have a meaning that is more precious
to me than I can explain.

But let me try to tell you this...

Saying "I care" means that I will always
  do everything I can to understand...

It means that you can trust me.
It means that you can tell me
  what's wrong.
It means that I will try to fix what I can,
that I will listen
  when you need me to hear, and that
— even in your most difficult moment —
  all you have to do is say the word,
    and your hand and my hand
      will not be apart.

It means that whenever you speak to me,
whether words are spoken through a smile
  or through a tear...
    I will listen with all my heart.

Hopes and Wishes

These are my hopes and my wishes...
That we may always be more than
   close; that nothing will come
   between the bond of love we share.
That I will always be there for you,
   as you will be for me.
That we will listen with love.

That we will share truths
   and treasured memories.
That we will trust and talk things out.
That we will understand.

That wherever you go, you will be
   in my heart,
and your hand will be
     in my hand.

What It Takes

It takes a certain kind of person to be special.

It takes someone who is really wonderful; someone who lights up this little corner of the world with feelings of friendship and love and understanding. It takes a truly unique personality and a knack for making life happier and more rewarding.

It takes someone who's willing to take the time.
It takes an individual who is able to open up
and share their innermost feelings with another.
It takes someone who makes the path of life an
easier and more beautiful journey. It takes a
rare combination of many qualities.

It takes a certain kind of person
to be special.

It takes someone
...exactly like you.

A Little Note
with a Lot of Love

Sometimes we need
reminders in our lives
of how much
people care.

If you ever get that feeling,
    I want you to remember this...

Beyond words that can even begin
to tell you how much,
    I hold you and your happiness
        within my heart each and
            every day.

I am so grateful for you and so thankful
to the years that have given me
so much to be thankful for.

I'm Going to Be Here for You, No Matter What

When you need someone to turn to, I'll be here for you. I will do whatever it takes and give as much as I can... to help you find your smile and get you back on steady ground again.

When you just need to talk, I will listen with my heart. And I will do my best to hear the things you may want to say, but can't quite find the words for.

I will never betray the trust you put in me. All I will do is keep on caring and doing my best to see you through. If there are decisions to be made, I may offer a direction to go in. If there are tears to be dried, I will tenderly dry them...

I want you to feel completely at ease about reaching out to me.

And don't ever forget this: You couldn't impose on me if you tried. It simply isn't possible.

Your happiness and peace of mind are so closely interwoven with mine that they are inseparable.

I will truly, deeply, and completely care
about you every day. You can count on that.

I hope it will invite a little more serenity into
your life to know you're not alone.

And I hope it will encourage a brighter day to
shine through.

I'm not going anywhere. I promise.

Unless it's to come to your side and
to hold out a hand... to you.

Just Thinking About You

I find myself thinking about you so much of the time...

About how lucky I am to have you as a part of my days; about what a good person you are; about everything you do for me, the obvious things and all the little things that you might not even know that you do... and about all the things you contribute to making my life nicer than it's ever been.

If someone were to ask me the secrets of happiness and gratitude and serenity, I know exactly what I'd do.

I'd tell them to make sure that they have a person in their life who's as precious, as special, and as wonderful... as you.

You're Appreciated More Than Words Can Say

Thank you so much... for taking the
  time to be there when I need you.
Thanks for helping to see me through
  so much.

Thank you for taking the hours
  out of your own precious days
to make a little more sunlight
  shine in mine.

Thank you for being a generous soul
    and a beautiful spirit
in a world that could use
    a million more people
just like you.

Thanks so much
    for everything you've done
and for all that you continue to do.

For All That You Are to Me

Having someone like you in my life is like having a wish come true.

You are a blessing and a miracle. You are a guiding light. You are a reminder that everything is all right. You and I are on the same wavelength; you always understand.

You know how I feel. You have insight into my very soul. You know the big and the little things. My highs and lows. My special dreams. You know where my Achilles' heel is, but that secret stays between us. You know what hurts and what helps, and you come to the rescue. When things aren't right, you throw me a rope and help me hang in there.

You and I share so much: Our shortcomings. Our highest hopes. Our serious thoughts. Our silliest jokes. You are where honesty comes from and where my wishes go when they don't want to be alone.

Being with you... is what it really means to feel at home.

It's Nice to Know That Some Things Will Never Change

No matter what is happening in the world.
No matter what worries or frustrations creep in.
No matter what glad or sad tidings come your way.
No matter how many bills come in the mail.
No matter how good or bad the news of the day.
No matter whether the weather is beautiful or not.
No matter how many times your smile gets lost.
No matter what is happening anywhere at any time...

You will always be in my thoughts. And I'll always be wishing I could find a way to remind you... that you are so important to me.

I know that life can be hard sometimes and that the world can be a crazy place. But I want you to remember that the two of us will always do what we can to make things better... and my very best wishes will be with you today, tomorrow, and forever.

Maybe You Can Do This Special Favor for Me...

Whenever we're apart,
I want you to keep me in your heart
and in your mind.

Just quietly close your eyes once in a while
and imagine me here, smiling and thinking
    such thankful thoughts of you.

For I spend so many quiet moments
    of my own
thinking how much I miss you,
    how hard it is to be apart,
        and how wonderful it is
            that you're always with me,
                here in my heart.

Special People

The special people in this world are the most precious and the most appreciated people of all. No matter what happens, they always understand. They go a million miles out of their way. They hold your hand.

They bring you smiles, when a smile is exactly what you need. They listen, and they hear what is said in the spaces between the words.

They care, and they let you know you're in their prayers.

Special people always know the perfect thing to do. They can make your whole day just by saying something that no one else could have said. Sometimes you feel like they share with you a secret language that others can't tune in to...

Special people can guide you, inspire you, comfort you, and light up your life with laughter. Special people understand your moods and nurture your needs, and they lovingly know just what you're after.

When your feelings come from deep inside and they need to be spoken to someone you don't have to hide from, you share them... with special people. When good news comes, special people are the first ones you turn to.

And when feelings overflow and tears
need to fall, special people help you
through it all.

Special people bring sunlight into your
life. They warm your world with their
presence, whether they are far away or
close by your side.

Special people are gifts
    that bring such happiness
and they're treasures
    that money can't buy.

I'm So Thankful That You're a Part of My Life

"Gratitude" is one of the nicest feelings a heart can have. It's a feeling that comes along for a very special reason — and it's a lovely thought that never goes away once it enters in. It joins together with precious memories and grateful hopes. Gratitude lives on, not for just a moment or a day, but through all the seasons that lie ahead.

My "thank you" feelings are especially sweet ones...
when it comes to thinking of all the things <u>you</u>
do. You deserve to receive so many smiles, such
an abundance of joys, and so much generosity —
reflected right back at you. That's why...

I hope you'll always remember my appreciation for
everything you've done
   ...and my endless gratitude.

I Don't Know What
I'd Do Without You

To you:

For keeping my spirits up.
For never letting me down.
For being here for me.
For knowing I'm there for you.

For bringing so many smiles my way.
For being sensitive to my needs.
For knowing just what to say.
For listening better than anyone else.

For bringing me laughter.
For bringing me light.
For understanding so much about me.
For trusting me with so much about you.

For being the best.
For being so beautiful.

    I don't know what I'd do
        ...without you.

Remember That You Can Always Count on Me

When life isn't easy and you wonder if anyone understands what you're going through, I want you... to reach out to me. Even if we find ourselves miles apart, don't ever forget that my heart is filled with so many hopes for your happiness.

I want you to feel like you can tell me everything that's on your mind. I want to be able to help you find a lot more smiles and make your days more joyful and filled with all the serenity you so dearly deserve...

When you wonder if there is anyone who cares completely and unconditionally, look my way. Let down your guard, and know that it's okay to bare your soul with someone who knows you as well as I do. When you need to talk things out, realize that you'll find a very loving listener... in me.

It doesn't matter what it's for; if it's important to you, then it's important to me. What matters most is that you gently remember:

Sometimes two heads (and two hearts)
are better than one can be, and you
can always count on me to be
there for you.

The Goodness You Give

This is for you, for being someone whose soul is so inspiring. This is a "thank you" for having a heart that's so big and a mind that is so open. And a spirit that I really love.

It's a message of gratitude for an incredibly special person. You inspire me with your wonderfulness. You're the first person I think of whenever I have something to share, and...

...you're the last person in the universe I would hurt or ever be unkind to. You are a treasure to my life, and I value you so much. You have an amazing knack for reassuring me.

You invite me to go along to the places your journeys take you when you dream, when you wonder, and when you reminisce...

And you let me know that you're a willing traveling companion, happy to join me in all my journeys, too.

I love that about you. I cherish the fact that you understand me so well and that I know you just about as well as I could ever know anyone.

I am blessed by the thousands of smiles we have shared, by the laughter that lingers in my heart, and by our concerns that have found a place of comfort in the sanctuary of our caring. I truly don't know what I'd do... without the goodness you give my life.

Everything and More

You are very important to me. And I'll try
   to tell you why...

You and I share so much of what is good about life.
Things like... so many experiences
   that only you and I have known.
And so many personal feelings and emotions
   that we have shown only to each other.

With us, the ordinary times turn into great times
and simple conversations turn into honest,
   trusting talks.

With us, so much is understood. So much is
    everything it should be... and more.

Laughter is natural and easy. Sentiment is shared.
Hard times are softened. And the more often I think
    about you, the more wonderful I realize you are.
Whether I'm alone or we're talking on the phone
    or we're taking a long walk,
I know how much we both care... and I cherish
    knowing that it will always be that way.

A Thousand Things

There are a thousand things
I would like to be for you...
but one of the most important
is just being
    the someone
       you can talk to.
There are so many things
    I would like
       to do for you.

There are so many things I would like
    to say and give and share.

But for today
    I just want you to know
that I promise:

I'll always be there,
    and I'll always care.

Everyone Needs Someone like You

Everyone needs someone who is
always there and always caring.
Everyone needs someone who is just a
touch or a card or a phone call away —
someone with whom you can share
everything that's in your heart
or simply talk about the day
in the way that only the two of you can.

Everyone needs someone to encourage them,
to believe in them, to give a pat on
the back when things have gone right
and a shoulder to cry on when they haven't.
Everyone needs someone to remind them
to keep trying and that it will all work out.

I hope everyone has someone
who's as wonderful as you.

Thank You for These Feelings

For bringing me happiness
as though it were a gift
I could open every day
...I am grateful to you.

For listening to the words
I want to say
...I appreciate you.

For letting me share the most
personal parts of your world
and for welcoming me with
your eyes
...I am indebted to you.

For being the wonderful, kind,
giving person you are
...I admire you.

For being everything you are to me
and for doing it so beautifully,
I thank you...
with all my heart.

It's So Nice Having Someone like You in My Life

I really want to sing your praises —
and let you know how important you
are to me and how wonderful you'll
always be.

I hope you'll forgive me for not telling
you that more often. You are the reason
for at least a million of my smiles,
and you've inspired some of the most
thankful thoughts I'll ever have.

I can't even begin to think about you without feeling an overwhelming sense of gratitude that someone so magnificent is a part of my life.

And just in case my golden opportunity to tell you that in person doesn't come along for a while... please keep this until it does... and let me say thanks,
     with all my heart,
          for everything about you.

Such a Blessing

In the course of a person's lifetime, there are so many prayers that get whispered and so many hopes that fill the heart. There are wishing stars that spend their entire evenings listening to all the things we long for.

I have said those prayers and had those hopes and chatted with more than my share of stars in the sky.

I always feel that if I ask and believe and wish well enough, some things are bound to turn out right.

But in all my prayers and wishes and hopes, I couldn't have asked for
     a blessing
          more wonderful
               than you in my life.

Remember This Always

With the deepest kind of gratitude and the sweetest kind of joy, I simply want to thank you for being all that you are to me.

You are truly amazing. Don't let anyone ever tell you otherwise. You are a treasure a million times more valuable than the ones some people spend a lifetime trying to find. You are a one-of-a-kind inspiration, someone whom anyone would be privileged to know.

And I am as proud as I can be... to know you
as well as I do.

So please... accept this special thanks and
remember it in all the days ahead, whether time
finds us far apart or it keeps us close together.

I want you to remember these words today...
and all the rest of forever.

You Touch My Life

It seems like I'm always searching
for a way to tell you
how wonderful I think you are.

And I thought that maybe
this book could help me
convey a few thoughts
    that I would love to share with you...

You're my definition of a special person.

I think you're fantastic.
And exceptional and unique and endearing.
To me, you're someone
who is very necessary to my well-being.
In so many ways, you fill my life
with happiness and the sweet feelings
of being so grateful and appreciative
    that you're here.

I could go on and on...
    but you get the picture.

I think you're a masterpiece.

A Place in My Heart

There will always be a special place in my heart... for you.

It is a place that knows how very much there is to appreciate about you. About your giving and your sharing. About your beautiful spirit and your kind and caring soul. About the generous way you manage to brighten so many days.

It is a place that recognizes your uniqueness
and that celebrates the meaning of all this. It
is a place that inspires a more positive outlook
on everything every time I think of you.

Within my heart is a place that is filled with
warm and thankful feelings...
    feelings that understand
       how seldom
          someone like you comes along.

If I Could Have a Wish Come True...

I would wish for nothing but wonderful things to come to you.

In your life, which is so precious to me, may troubles, worries, and problems never linger; may they only make you that much stronger and able and wise.

And may you rise each day with sunlight
in your heart, success in your path,
answers to your prayers,
   and that smile
      — that I love to see —
         always there... in your eyes.

You Are the Best

Your wonderful qualities have made
a lasting impression on me that I
    will admire for as long as I live.

You give me so much to be thankful for.

You have wisdom that goes beyond
your words, a sweetness that goes
beyond your smile, and a heart
    of pure gold.

You take the time to hear my deepest
thoughts, my feelings, and my fears.

You've dried tears no one else could see,
you've helped me find happiness,
    and you've taught me that I really can
        make some of my dreams come true.

This Very Special Prayer Is for You...

For happiness, so deserving. For sweet contentment. For quiet serenity. For everything gracious and good.

It's a prayer of thanks for wonderful friendships and for loving families. It's a prayer of appreciation for all the blessings that come to us so beautifully.

It's a prayer for seeing your way through any challenges and changes that life brings to your days. It's a prayer for health and understanding. For gentle roads to walk along.

It's a prayer for making every day as precious as it can be. It's a prayer for you to be safe and strong. Encouraged by the steps you take. Embraced by every beautiful memory you've ever made. And warmed by every reason to hope.

In all the days ahead, I hope you will keep this prayer in your heart. It's a prayer for God to always smile on you and for the days in the life that you are living... to be so kind and so giving.

Things I Treasure

I have loved every day we have shared. I have cherished every memory we've made.

I have appreciated the uniqueness and the sweetness and the wonder of you more than my words can ever say.

What a beautiful soul you have, and what a blessing you are.

I am so grateful to you for giving me such a wealth of things to treasure.

Thank you for the precious feelings and the priceless moments. Thank you for an amazing amount of encouragement and understanding. Thank you for the comfort of feeling so close to you and for letting me know I can always count on you.

Thank you for all the gifts you've given, all the smiles you've inspired, and all the things you've always done to make my life... such a wonderful one.

Thoughts for You

One of the most special places in my heart
   will always be saved for you.

You...
      the one person I can always talk to;
      the one person who understands.

You...
      for making me laugh in the rain;
      for helping me shoulder my troubles.

You...
for loving me in spite of myself
and always putting me
back on my feet again.

You...
for giving me someone to believe in;
someone who lets me know that
there really is goodness and kindness
and laughter and love in the world.

You...
for being one of the best
parts of my life and proving it
over and over again.

In This World

There are a few absolute gems in this world. They are the people who make a tremendous difference in other people's lives... with the smiles they give, the blessings they share, and the way they warm the hearts of everyone around them.

Those rare and remarkable people are so deserving of every hope and happiness. They are the people who are incredibly unique, enormously thanked, and endlessly appreciated for everything they do.

And one of those wonderful, deserving, and one-of-a-kind people is most definitely... you.

Just Between Us

I don't think it would be possible
for me to be more thankful or more
appreciative of all that you are.

You are such a nice part of my life!

If it weren't for you, I wouldn't have
half as much laughter or nearly as
much joy. I wouldn't have as much
peace or understanding. And I definitely
wouldn't have as much fun!

I love that you're here. And whether it's in person or on the phone... I love the connection that is always there between us.

What we share is really something special. I feel more at home with you than I do with just about anyone, and feelings like those are some of the most precious of all.

How Blessed I Am to Have You in My Life

If you could see yourself reflected in my eyes, you would see someone who makes my heart just smile inside. You would catch a glimpse of somebody who has been such a wonderful influence on my life and who keeps on making a beautiful difference in my days.

If you could hear the words I would love to share, you would be able to listen to a special tribute to you, one that sings your praises, speaks of an unending gratitude, and describes how much I'll always appreciate you.

If you could imagine one of the nicest gifts anyone could ever receive, you would begin to understand what your presence in my life has meant to me.

I Wish for You

Happiness. Deep down within.

Serenity. With each sunrise.

Success. In each facet of your life.

Close and caring friends.

Love. That never ends.

Special memories. Of all the yesterdays.

A bright today. With so much to be thankful for.

A path. That leads to beautiful tomorrows.

Dreams. That do their best to come true.

And appreciation. Of all the wonderful
things about you.

You Are a
Very Special Person

I want you to know how amazing you are.
I want you to know how much you're
treasured and celebrated and quietly thanked.

I want you to feel really good...
    about who you are.
About all the great things you do!

I want you to appreciate your uniqueness.
Acknowledge your talents and abilities.
Realize what a beautiful soul you have.
Understand the wonder within.

You make so much sun shine through,
and you inspire so much joy in the lives of
everyone who is lucky enough to know you.

You are a very special person, giving so
many people a reason to smile...

You deserve to receive the best in return, and one of my heart's favorite hopes is that the happiness you give away will come back to warm you each and every day of your life.

I Think the World of You

Do you know what you are?
You are one of the most special
people I will ever have the privilege
of knowing.

I really mean that. The older I get,
the more I understand how rare it is
to be blessed with someone like you...

You're unique in so many ways, and there are very few things in life that even come close to bringing me as much happiness as you do.

You never cease to amaze me. There are so many moments when I am quietly in awe of you... of the joy you inspire, of the serenity you share, and of all the great things that just seem to naturally be a part of you.

It's so easy and so nice... being with you. It opens my eyes to all the wonderful qualities about you. I see goodness and kindness there. I see compassion and understanding.

And I never fail to see a twinkle in your eyes... a gentle reminder to me that I am in the company of someone who has a big heart and a beautiful ability to make each day a good one...

I know you're probably going to feel a little embarrassed to hear all the praises I am singing about you, but you deserve all these praises... and many, many more. I'll always think the world of you.

I'll cherish all the memories and
appreciate the closeness and thank
my lucky stars for everything.

So please... don't ever forget:

I think you are one of the
most precious people
this world will ever be
blessed with.

About the Author

Best-selling author and editor
Douglas Pagels has inspired
millions of readers with his
insights and his anthologies.
No one is better at touching
on so many subjects that are
deeply personal and truly
universal at the same time.

His writings have been translated into over a dozen
languages due to their global appeal and inspiring outlook
on life, and his work has been quoted by many worthy
causes and charitable organizations.

He and his wife live in Colorado, and they are the parents
of children in college and beyond. Over the years, Doug has
spent much of his time as a classroom volunteer, a youth
basketball coach, an advocate for local environmental issues,
a frequent traveler, and a craftsman, building a cabin in the
Rocky Mountains.